The INDIANAPOLIS 500

Published by Creative Education, Inc.
123 South Broad Street, Mankato, MN 56001

Designed by Rita Marshall with the help of Thomas Lawton
Cover illustration by Rob Day, Lance Hidy Associates

Copyright © 1990 by Creative Education, Inc.
Photography by Allsport, Focus on Sports, Indianapolis
Motor Speedway Corporation, Buck Miller, Third Coast
Stock Source

Printed in the United States

Library of Congress Cataloging-in-Publication Data

Weber, Bruce.
   The Indianapolis 500/by Bruce Weber: edited by Michael E.
Goodman.
    p.   cm.—(Great moments in sports)
    Summary: Discusses the history, the cars, and the drivers of
America's biggest racing event.
    ISBN 0-88682-321-8: $11.95
    1. Indianapolis Speedway Race—History—Juvenile
literature.   2. Automobile racing drivers—United States—Biography
—Juvenile literature.   [1. Indianpolis Speedway Race—
History.]   I. Goodman, Michael E.   II. Title.   III. Title:
Indianapolis Five Hundred.   IV. Series.
GV1033.5.I55W43   1989   89-36706
796.7'2'0922—dc19   CIP
[B]   AC

The INDIANAPOLIS 500

BRUCE WEBER

CREATIVE EDUCATION INC.

It's a festival of color, smells, and noise. More than 300,000 auto racing fans holler away, as firecrackers explode overhead, bands play, and singers perform. Behind all this noise is the steady hum of thirty-three well-tuned engines of the world's fastest race cars.

These cars and their drivers, the hundreds of thousands of spectators packing the grandstands and infield of the racetrack, and the millions of people watching the race on television around the world are part of America's biggest racing event—the Indianapolis 500.

The race is held every year on Memorial Day. It is the most famous automobile race in the United States and attracts larger crowds than any single sporting event in America.

By the time the sun rises over Indianapolis, Indiana, on race day, the track is already busy. The gates to the giant speedway open at 6:00 A.M., but fans have been arriving for several days. Thousands have been staying in a campground just behind the track to await the race.

In all, more than a quarter of a million fans will have seats in the grandstands, and others will pay around ten dollars apiece for a space on the infield. They may be able to see the race—or they may not. They don't care, as long as they can take part in the festive atmosphere.

On the night before the race, the annual Festival Parade is held.

For true "Indy" fans, race day ends a month-long celebration of speed. The drivers, their teams of mechanics and helpers, and their sleek cars arrive in late April. Three weeks before the big race, opening ceremonies are followed by the first on-track practice runs. With two weeks to go, the first time trials draw all of the attention. Only the swiftest thirty-three cars and drivers will qualify for the race. The fastest driver on the first day of the time trials wins the desirable pole position—number one in the first row.

Practices continue daily, with qualifying runs on the weekends until the week of the race. Once the field of thirty-three is set, there is a three-day break, followed by a final week of speed work on the track.

Everything about Indy weekend is big. A minimarathon in downtown Indianapolis draws more than 7,000 runners. The Queen's Ball, which honors the queen of the festival, packs the house. The night before the race, more than 300,000 spectators line the streets of Indianapolis for the annual Festival Parade. And then it's race day.

The race starts precisely at 11:00 a.m., weather permitting.

8

The drivers fit snugly into their powerful cars. The final adjustments are made, and the track loudspeakers boom the famous words: "Gentlemen, start your engines." Weather permitting, the green flag falls at exactly 11:00 A.M. The grueling, often dangerous 500-mile journey to fame and fortune is on.

Squeezed into the cockpit, the drivers become part of the machine.

9

HOW INDY BEGAN

The Indianapolis 500 wasn't always such a spectacular event. The early days of the Indy track were a disaster. Four men built the track over a bean field in 1909, using crushed stone and tar. It opened on August 19 for three days of racing that were a horror show, with accidents all over the track.

The owners knew that safety was vital for racing, so they decided to pave the track. They brought in 3,200,000 paving bricks and rebuilt it. By December 1909, the new track was ready, but the weather wasn't—it was too cold. In 1910, however, short races were run in May, July, and September. That set the scene for the first 500-mile race.

Some things in sports turn out to be perfect almost by accident. The ninety feet between bases in baseball are just right. The ten yards for a first down in football are on target. They just worked out right. The same is true of the 500-mile distance for the Indianapolis auto race. The track owners decided on the distance. It was long enough to make a good test for cars and drivers but not so long that spectators would get bored. The owners also picked Memorial Day, May 30, for their race. Both choices turned out to be perfect ones.

Ray Harroun won the first Indianapolis 500 in 1911.

More than 80,000 fans packed the Indianapolis Motor Speedway for the first Indy 500 in 1911. The track operators had placed 3,000 hitching posts outside to allow fans who arrived on horseback to tie up their horses during the race.

Forty cars ran in the first Indy. Ray Harroun won it. His six-cylinder Marmon "Yellow Jacket" thundered around the track at 74.6 MPH. Though some drivers go that fast on highways today, the speed was incredible in 1911. The fans loved it, and a tradition was born.

Except for 1917 and 1918 (during World War I) and the years during World War II, the Indy 500 has been an American fixture every May. Rain has shortened the race five times for safety reasons. The shortest was 255 miles in 1976. In 1916, the race was scheduled for only 300 miles to save gas and tires.

The early Indy 500s featured daredevil amateur drivers in leather helmets. Their cars were huge, clumsy-looking machines. Today's sleek racing "bullets," driven by professionals, are far different. The one thing that never changes, however, is the competition. It is fierce. Fractions of a second can mean the difference between winning and losing.

The Indy tradition born in 1911 continues today.

AT THE BRICKYARD

The Indy 500 is special, and so is the track on which it is run. They call the Indianapolis Motor Speedway "the Greatest Race Course in the World." Few auto racing experts would disagree.

Much has changed, however, since the first race on tar and crushed stone in 1909. The first all-brick track followed seven months later. In 1937, parts of the track were paved with asphalt, which made the road smoother and the track faster. Then, in 1976 and 1988, nearly the entire track was paved with asphalt. Still, a one-yard strip at the starting line features the original bricks. That is why they call Indy "the Brickyard."

Even though there were no races during World War I, the Speedway wasn't idle. It was used to repair planes, and the infield served as a landing strip for military planes. More than 100 acres around the raceway were used for planting hay

Pit crew practice during Speed Week.

The original stands, made of wood, were used until World War II. No high school football field would use such rickety stands today. By the mid-1940s, the Speedway was in terrible shape. There were holes and cracks all along the track, and weeds and high grass between the bricks. The owner considered shutting down the track for good.

Indiana businessman Tony Hulman bought the track and made three-time winner Wilbur Shaw its president. "I can't imagine Indiana without the Indy 500," Hulman said. "Just like I can't imagine Kentucky without the Kentucky Derby." Together, Hulman and Shaw set out to save Indy.

They had a long-range plan. Step one was to get rid of the old wooden stands. Gradually, they were replaced by sleek concrete and shiny steel structures. An office and museum building went up inside the main gate in 1956, and the control tower was rebuilt in 1957.

Except for the thirty-six-inch-wide strip at the starting line, all of the bricks were gone by 1961, the fiftieth anniversary of the first Indy 500 race. The stands were also enlarged so that more fans could watch the race in comfort. Today, more than 300,000 can fit into Indy.

The track has been paved several times, creating a faster, smoother course.

The Indianapolis Motor Speedway is a jewel. When the folks who run Indy brag that theirs is "the Greatest Race Course in the World," they just may be right.

THE EARLY DAYS

Ever since the early days of the Indy 500, races at "the Brickyard" have always provided great moments for the spectators. One of the most unusual races occurred during the second Indy race in 1912.

Ralph DiPalma and his Mercedes were comfortably leading near the end of the race. "It's over," thought many of the 80,000 in the stands, and they began to leave.

Other than rubber tires, Danny Sullivan's modern race car (at right) bears little resemblance to Joe Dawson's 1912 winner.

Suddenly, DiPalma's car started slowing. One of the car's connecting rods had broken, and it began moving slower and slower. Finally, on the 199th lap of the 200-lap race, less than three miles from the finish, the Mercedes stopped completely. DiPalma and his mechanic, who was riding with him, tried to push the car, but they were not nearly fast enough. Local favorite Joe Dawson rushed past DiPalma to win the race. Dawson didn't stay around long for a victory celebration. Instead, he drove home to tell his mother what had happened. She was more concerned with her son's safety than his victory, however. "At least you didn't get hurt," she said.

DiPalma nearly lost a second time in 1915. He took the lead early and extended it. He was lucky he had a big lead because by the 197th lap, his car began to slow down. Again a broken connecting rod was the problem. This time the car kept running, however. DiPalma finally won the 500, by just three and a half minutes!

Gaston Chevrolet provided another great memory when he won the 1920 Indy 500. It was the first time an American had won the race in an American car since Joe Dawson's miracle finish in 1912. It was also the first time an Indy 500 winner drove the whole race on one set of tires. Chevrolet had built and entered several cars in the race. The other Chevrolet cars had dropped out earlier when their steering arms broke. While Gaston was celebrating his victory, he leaned against the steering arm on his car. It broke, too.

Gaston Chevrolet drove to victory using just one set of tires in 1920.

Pete DePaolo won the Indy 500 in 1925, becoming the first man to average over 100 MPH for the race. His mark of 101.13 MPH lasted for seven years. He also started an Indy tradition. DePaolo was the nephew of the 1915 winner, Ralph DiPalma. This marked the first time two family members had won the race. The story of the Indy "family" tradition has added several more chapters through the years.

Another exciting race occurred in 1937 and featured the man who later became the track president, Wilbur Shaw. Shaw was far ahead late in the race when his car's oil pressure began to drop dangerously. What should he do? He could head for the pits, where the mechanics were, and give up the lead. Or he could take his chances, hoping that the oil wouldn't run out and ruin his engine.

Shaw cut his speed and allowed runner-up Ralph Hepburn to gain ground. With only ten miles to go, Hepburn was less than a mile behind. Shaw continued to crawl along, and Hepburn kept closing the gap. By the time they reached the final turn in the last lap, Hepburn trailed by just a few feet. Quickly, Shaw pushed down the accelerator and held off his opponent by two seconds for the win. Shaw later captured the 1939 and 1940 Indys to become the first driver ever to win consecutive races.

DANGER MADE SAFER

Safety was a concern for early Indy champions such as Dawson, DiPalma, and Shaw, and has continued to be of importance throughout Indy history. Car racing can be a very dangerous sport; that is part of its thrill. But race car drivers and builders have done much to make driving safer for both racers and everyday drivers.

For the first twenty races, most Indy cars contained two men: the driver and the racing mechanic. The mechanic was on hand to deal with engine problems. He also served as the driver's assistant, looking out for traffic coming up from behind. A few Indy cars used a rearview mirror. That invention helped drivers complete the race safely, and it has helped both race-car and passenger-car drivers ever since.

Fire is the racer's greatest enemy. The link between fire and death has haunted Indy and every other racetrack in the world. Fire prevention was a major goal when the United States Auto Club was created in 1956 to govern racing in America. USAC rules were passed to make racing safer. Almost everything a driver wears is fireproof or fire retardant. Each driver's uniform costs about $1,500, but that is a small price to pay for safety.

In 1965, fuel cells that help prevent the spread of fire during a crash were made a requirement. The forty-gallon fuel cell is installed behind the driver, who is protected in the "tub." Also, no gasoline is used at Indy. It has been replaced with methanol, an alcohol-based fuel, which is less likely to burst into flames.

Refueling crew members wear complete safety gear.

Safety helmets were first used in 1932. Beginning three years later, everyone had to wear them. Today's helmets are made of fiberglass with a polystyrene liner. The price tag: around $1,000.

Al Unser, Jr. depends on his fiberglass helmet for protection.

The first seat belts began appearing at about the same time as helmets. Many drivers refused to wear them at first because they thought the belts might slow down their ability to escape from a burning car. When the famed driver Rex Mays was killed after being thrown from his car in 1949, more drivers began to wear belts. By the mid-1950s, they were also required equipment. Today, drivers wear belts and shoulder harnesses, and both have saved many lives.

Indy racing not only has entertained people over the years, it has also contributed much to the cars driven on American highways. Four-wheel brakes and hydraulic shock absorbers were first used at Indy. Disk brakes started there, too. Low-pressure and oversized tires were developed for Indy cars. The Brickyard has helped make driving safer everywhere and the great moments in car racing much more enjoyable.

THE AJ DECADE

Fans flock to the Indy 500 every year for the speed and danger that are part of the race. But they also come to cheer for special heroes. One of the greatest of these is Anthony Joseph Foyt, known simply as "AJ." Since 1958 AJ has been there every time the green flag has fallen, and four times he has been first when the checkered flag has come down. Only Al Unser, Sr., has enjoyed as many trips into Victory Lane.

Safety belts have saved many lives throughout the years.

Almost everyone in racing loves and respects AJ. He is a tremendously hard worker. He goes all out to win every time, and hates to "settle" for second place.

Foyt, shown during the 1989 race, nearly lost in '61 because of a pit stop.

Foyt was lucky to win his first Indy in 1961. AJ led Eddie Sachs by ten full seconds late in the race and figured to win easily. But then his crew ordered him into the pit. His fuel gauge had failed on his last pit stop, and the crew thought he might run out of fuel. As Foyt waited for his tank to be filled in the pit area, Sachs sped past and into the lead.

Sachs sailed on, well ahead of Foyt. Then, with about five laps to go, Sachs felt his car jump. Rubber began peeling off his right rear tire. What could he do? If he kept going, he might hang on for the win. However, if the tire blew, he would lose control. It was a tough decision. Sachs chose safety and pulled into the pit area. This choice allowed Foyt to regain the lead and earn his first Indy win.

Following a 69th-lap wreck that knocked him out of the race in 1962 and a third-place finish in 1963, Foyt was back on top in 1964. Unfortunately, it was a race filled with tragedy. Fire claimed the lives of both 1961's hard-luck loser Eddie Sachs and Dave Mc-Donald. Two other drivers barely escaped fires in their cars. Parnelli Jones was leading the race when a freak spark sent his car into flames as he was taking

on fuel, but he managed to get away just in time. Scotland's Jim Clark saw the rear end of his Lotus disappear in flame, but he was unhurt. Foyt's victory in this danger-filled race was a combination of skill, courage, and luck. But it was also filled with sorrow because of the loss of some of his fellow racers.

"I don't make close friends in racing anymore," said a saddened Foyt after the race. "It's too tough to lose them."

Each driver depends on his pit crew.

A broken gearbox knocked Foyt out of the 1965 Indy, and an eleven-car wreck he was involved in at the start of the 1966 race ended his day early. Then came 1967. AJ was leading after 199 laps and he could almost taste his third Indy win. He had already received the white flag that signals one lap to go for the leader. Then AJ noticed trouble ahead of him. Several cars had collided and were stopped along the inside of the track at all angles. AJ used some nifty driving to get around the stalled cars, like a football running back avoiding tacklers, and sailed across the finish line unharmed and victorious.

With three wins in seven years, A. J. Foyt owned the decade of the 1960s, providing many great moments at the Indianapolis Motor Speedway.

Ground-hugging auto design has led to higher speeds.

INDY'S GREATEST FAMILY

The Indy 500 has always been a mixture of triumph and tragedy for A. J. Foyt and racing's other great drivers. One family has shared the most triumph and tragedy at Indy—the Unsers.

27

The Unsers from Albuquerque, New Mexico, have truly been the "royal family" of auto racing for more than seventy-five years. Al Unser, Sr., who has won at Indy four times, may be the most famous member of the clan, but his dad, Jerry, started the wheels rolling back in the 1910s. Jerry and his brothers Lou and Joe drove motorcycles to the top of Colorado's Pike's Peak. And that was before a road had even been built there!

Jerry Unser, Jr. was the first Unser to compete in the Indy 500.

The three brothers all planned to enter Indy in 1929. But Joe was killed testing a car on a Colorado highway, and the dream of winning at Indy was postponed until the next Unser generation.

Al's oldest brother, Jerry, Jr., became the first Unser to race at Indy, though his start in the 1958 event ended almost as soon as it began. A fifteen-car collision on the first lap knocked Jerry out of the race. The following year, he was killed in a crash during a practice run at Indy.

Still, the Unsers continued to race. Al Unser, Sr., drove to a second-place finish in the 1967 Indy 500. In 1968, both Al and brother Bobby were entered at Indy. Midway through the race, Al's car lost two wheels and bounced off a wall. Luckily, he wasn't hurt, but he was through for the day. He climbed to the top of the wall and waved to Bobby. "I'm okay," he shouted. Bobby was reassured and brought home the Unser family's first Indy victory.

Al was injured and missed the 1969 race, but he came back strong the next year. His practice sessions were perfect: so was the qualifying run. Al finished first and earned the pole position for the race.

From the pits it was clear that the Unsers were true champions.

On Memorial Day in 1970, Al faced his brother, along with thirty-one other challengers, including Johnny Rutherford, Mark Donahue, and A. J. Foyt. Foyt dropped out early, and none of the others really threatened. Al led for 190 of the 200 laps and was in control all the way. When his "Johnny Lightning Special" turned into Victory Lane, there was Bobby waiting with a handshake and a hug. He was the first to congratulate his little brother.

Al Unser, Sr. has won the Indy a record-tying four times.

Al won again the next year with a new car. It marked the first back-to-back Indy victories since Bill Vukovich won in both 1953 and 1954. Just to prove he was no "two-year wonder," Al won again in 1978 and 1987, to tie A. J. Foyt as Indy's two most-successful racers. Bobby also continued the family's winning tradition with triumphs in 1975 and 1981.

Now Al Unser, Jr., the man they call "Little Al," is ready to make his move at Indy. At age twenty, he became the youngest driver ever to break the 200-mile-per-hour barrier in practice runs before the 1983 race. He was also one of the top qualifiers in 1987. The Unser name should continue to provide great moments at Indy for decades to come.

HERE'S TO THE WINNERS

What keeps the Unsers, A. J. Foyt, and the other great racers coming back to Indy each year, despite the dangers? Part of the answer has to be the thrill of speed. Throughout history people have been trying to go faster and faster—on foot, on horseback, on skis, on bicycles, or in racing cars.

The thrill of speed has brought racers back to Indy year after year.

When Ray Harroun "sped" to victory at 75 MPH in the first Indy 500 in 1911, he could not have dreamed that someday a driver would go 200 MPH hour as Al Unser, Jr., did seventy-two years later. New technology and better driving techniques have made it possible for racers to go faster and faster in their magnificent driving machines.

Those magnificent machines are another reason for the popularity of auto racing. The car is a man-made invention, and there is a special thrill that comes from building and piloting the fastest car in America's greatest race.

Still, the main reason for Indy's popularity is winning. Winning at Indy takes skill, strength, and perseverance. It also takes great teamwork—from the driver and the car designers to the mechanics and the pit crews. The cup for winning at Indy is not presented just to A. J. Foyt or Al Unser but to the "Foyt team" or the "Unser team." They are all winners.

Indy is all of these things—speed, sleek and powerful machines, and winners. That's what makes it America's biggest festival. That's why thirty-three drivers and more than 300,000 fanatical fans pack the Indianapolis Motor Speedway every Memorial Day to take part in some of racing's greatest moments.

Superior teamwork is a requirement for every Indy victory.